W9-BYQ-467

EARLY PEOPLES

INDIANS OF THE NORTHWEST COAST AND PLATEAU

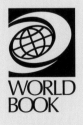

WORLD
BOOK

World Book
a Scott Fetzer company
Chicago
www.worldbookonline.com

World Book, Inc.
233 N. Michigan Avenue
Chicago, IL 60601
U.S.A.

For information about other World Book publications, visit our
Web site at http://www.worldbookonline.com or call
1-800-WORLDBK (967-5325).
For information about sales to schools and libraries, call
1-800-975-3250 (United States), or 1-800-837-5365 (Canada).

Library of Congress Cataloging-in-Publication Data

Indians of the Northwest Coast and Plateau.
    p. cm. -- (Early peoples)
    Includes index.
    Summary: "A discussion of the Indians of the Northwest Coast and Plateau,
including who the people were, where they lived, the rise of civilization, social
structure, religion, art and architecture, science and technology, daily life,
entertainment and sports, and fall of civilization. Features include timelines,
fact boxes, glossary, list of recommended readings and web sites, and index"
--Provided by publisher.
    ISBN 978-0-7166-2137-9
    1. Indians of North America--Northwest, Pacific--Juvenile literature.
I. World Book, Inc.
    E78.N77I55 2009
    979.504'97--dc22

                                                    2008024770

Printed in China by Leo Paper Products Ltd.,
Heshan, Guangdong
2nd printing June 2010

STAFF

TABLE OF CONTENTS

Glossary There is a glossary on pages 60-61. Terms defined in the glossary are in type **that looks like this** on their first appearance on any spread (two facing pages).

Additional Resources Books for further reading and recommended Web sites are listed on page 62. Because of the nature of the Internet, some Web site addresses may have changed since publication. The publisher has no responsibility for any such changes or for the content of cited sources.

WHO WERE THE INDIANS OF THE NORTHWEST COAST AND PLATEAU CULTURAL AREAS?

American Indians have lived in North America for thousands of years. Scholars know little about the early times of these first Americans. **Archaeologists** have pieced together some of the early story of the American Indians by studying the remains of the people and their culture. Pottery, stone tools, animal bones, charcoal from campfires—all have offered clues about how and when the early Indians lived. But many questions remain unanswered.

Scientists believe that **Paleo-Indians**, the first people known to live in North America, probably arrived around 13,500 years ago. Evidence suggests that at least 9,000 years ago, people began living along the Northwest coast of North America, in the area along the Pacific Ocean that spans from southern Alaska to northern California. More than 6,000 years ago, the **tribes** of the Plateau **cultural** area arrived in their territory. This area stretches from southern British Columbia in present-day Canada down through parts of present-day Washington, Oregon, Idaho, Montana, and into northern California.

Neither the Northwest coast nor the Plateau cultural areas held a single, unified group of Indians in these early times. Groups in both areas shared similar customs and ways of life. In both areas, the people were hunter-gatherers who lived in small villages.

◄ A carved sculpture that once stood at the entrance to a Haida longhouse on the Queen Charlotte Islands in Canada. Indians of the Northwest coast are famous for their woodcarvings. These carvings include masks and **totem** poles, such as the totem pole shown in the background.

WHO WERE THE INDIANS OF THE NORTHWEST
COAST AND PLATEAU CULTURAL AREAS?

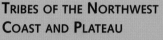

5

A Rich Coastal Culture

The people of the Northwest coast lived in an environment where food and other resources were much more plentiful than in many other regions of North America. Many of the festivals and traditions of the Indians of the Northwest coast region included displays of wealth. They also had a strong sense of family history.

Life on the Plateau

For the groups who lived in the Plateau cultural area near the coast, their traditional way of life centered on fishing, particularly for salmon. They also hunted small game and gathered roots and berries.

Some Plateau Indians who lived farther inland adopted many of the practices of neighboring Plains Indians. The men of the interior Plateau tribes hunted buffalo and other large game on horseback, and these Plateau families lived in tipis (also spelled tepees) made of animal skins.

TRIBES OF THE NORTHWEST COAST AND PLATEAU

Tribes of the Northwest coast cultural area included:
Bella Coola (*BEHL uh KOO luh*)
Chinook (*chuh NOOK or chuh NUK*)
Coast Salish (a number of tribes on the coast who spoke Salish languages)
Haida (*HY duh*)
Kwakiutl (*KWAH kee OO tuhl*)
Nootka (*NOOT kuh*)
Tlingit (*TLIHNG giht*)
Tsimshian (*TSIHM shee uhn*)

Tribes of the northern Plateau cultural area included:
Coeur d'Alene (*KUR duh LAYN*)
Flathead
Kutenai (*KOO tuh nay*)
Lillooet (*LIHL WEHT*)
Okanagan (*OH kuh NAHG uhn*)
Shuswap (*SHOO swahp*)
Spokane (*spoh KAN*)
Thompson (*TOMP suhn*)

Tribes of the southern Plateau cultural area included:
Cayuse (*ky YOOS*)
Nez Perce (*nehz PURS*)
Palouse (*pah LOOS*)
Umatilla (*YOO muh TIHL uh*)
Walla Walla (*WOL uh WOL uh*)
Yakima (*YAK uh mah*)

◄ A group of Flathead Indians and an interpreter (top, center), shown in a photograph taken in 1884. The Flathead were given that name by other Indians in the region. Many Indians in the Northwest shaped the head of an infant by applying pressure to the skull over time. The Flathead did not practice head shaping. To Indians who did, their heads looked flat.

A Land of Plenty

The Indians of the Northwest coast and Plateau **cultural** areas lived in different environments. Both groups, however, lived in areas that generally had plenty of food and other natural resources, though late winter could be a time of hunger on the Plateau.

▶ The Northwest coast cultural area is shown in pink. Some of the **tribes** from this region are located on this map.

▼ The Columbia Plateau offered an abundance of resources to the Indians who lived in the region. Lakes were teeming with water birds and fish; the forested mountain slopes provided acorns, game animals, and even clothing and shelter.

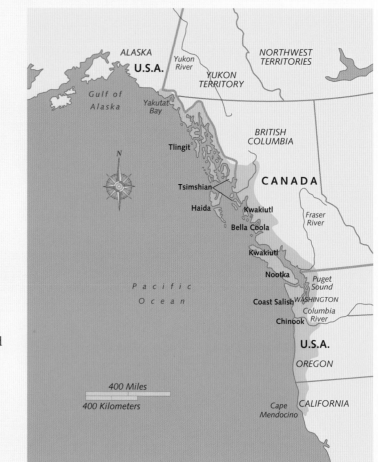

ALASKA
U.S.A.
Yukon River
NORTHWEST TERRITORIES
YUKON TERRITORY
Gulf of Alaska
Yakutat Bay
BRITISH COLUMBIA
Tlingit
Tsimshian
CANADA
Haida
Kwakiutl
Bella Coola
Fraser River
Kwakiutl
Nootka
Puget Sound
Pacific Ocean
Coast Salish WASHINGTON
Chinook
Columbia River
U.S.A.
OREGON
400 Miles
400 Kilometers
Cape Mendocino
CALIFORNIA

Life on the Coast

The Northwest coast cultural area is a narrow strip of land along the Pacific Ocean. The territory stretches about 2,000 miles (3,200 kilometers) from north to south, through parts of what are now Alaska, British Columbia, Washington, Oregon, and northern California. The area also includes offshore islands.

The Northwest coast cultural area has a moist, relatively warm climate, and it is home to huge evergreen forests. The Northwest coast Indians used the giant cedars that grew in the forests for many of their needs—including housing, transportation, clothing, and blankets. The forests and plentiful waterways in the area were also home to many sources of food, including plants, fish, and game animals.

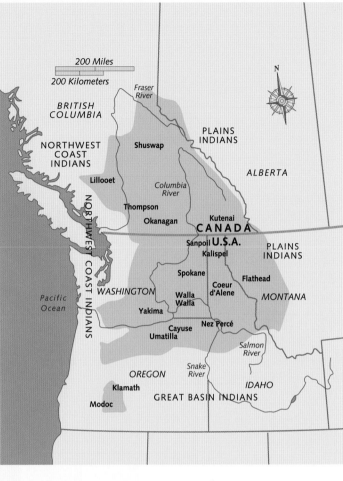

▲ The Plateau cultural area is shown in pink. Some of the tribes from this region are located on this map.

A Land of Rivers

The Plateau cultural area is so named because it includes the Columbia Plateau—the flat plain through which the Columbia River flows. The Columbia River is 1,243 miles (2,000 kilometers) long, one of the longest rivers in North America. The Plateau cultural area includes parts of present-day British Columbia and Alberta and the states of Washington, Oregon, Idaho, and Montana. It also includes a small section of northern California. The western boundary of the region is formed by the Cascade Mountains. The Rocky Mountains form its eastern boundary.

The Plateau cultural area contains excellent sources of both food and water. The Columbia River connects the Snake and Salmon rivers to the Pacific Ocean. The Columbia also has many tributaries (small streams that feed into a larger stream or river). The Plateau Indians lived along the many waterways in the area. They were able to catch fish in the rivers and streams, and hunt for game and gather plants in the surrounding meadows and forests.

FISHERMEN IN ANCIENT TIMES

Archaeologists have discovered ancient fish bones, hooks, and nets at a site on the Columbia River in Oregon. The find revealed that people have been fishing in the area since at least 7,500 B.C.

Indian Society

Family ties were extremely important for Indians of the Northwest coast and Plateau **cultural** areas. The way that a person was related to other members of the **tribe** affected every part of his or her life.

Family Groups

Among the Northwest coast and Plateau Indians, the basic unit of society was the **extended family**. Further units of society existed for these Indians. For example, a **band** was made up of several extended families related by blood and marriage that lived in an area.

In the Northwest coast groups, **clans** (groups of extended families that share a common ancestor in the distant past) were also important units of society. Every clan had a symbol—a representation of the spirit, usually an animal, which had, according to **legend**, helped the first members of the clan. Most northern groups of Northwest coast Indians split their clans into two groups, each called a **moiety** *(MOY uh tee).*

Clan members within a certain tribe might be blood relatives. But some clans existed in more than one tribe. For example, the Haida and Tlingit both had Raven clans. Although the Haida and Tlingit Ravens were not related to each other by blood, they considered themselves related because they shared a clan. Because marriage between members of the same clan was forbidden, men and women from the Haida and Tlingit Ravens could not marry.

Clan Rights

Clans played an important role among the Indians of the Northwest coast. Clan membership determined a person's **status** in the group. Clan members inherited wealth, titles (such as chief), and many rights from their relatives. Inherited rights could even include the right to sing certain songs or to fish in certain areas.

▶ A wooden model depicts a Tsimshian clan chief wearing his clan's **totem**. Totems were a part of everyday life for Indians of the Northwest coast. For these groups, totems often symbolized a person's clan. Totems were carved into weapons and wooden headdresses and used as decorations on clothing and crafts.

Blood Lines

Among the northern tribes of Northwest coast Indians, such as the Haida, Tlingit, and Tsimshian, children belonged to their mother's clan. This is called a **matrilineal** *(mat ruh LIHN ee uhl)* system. Among the more southern tribes, clan membership was traced through the father's side. This is called a **patrilineal** *(pat ruh LIHN ee uhl)* system. The Coast Salish and Kwakiutl peoples shared the **heritage** of both sides of their families.

Most of the Plateau Indians followed a patrilineal system. A person's family was with his or her father's people. In the case of the Yakima, however, both sides of a person's family were considered blood relatives.

▲ Totem poles in a Nimkish village in Alert Bay, British Columbia, in about 1900. The images carved into the poles depict the clan totems of both of the parents of the owner of the poles. The photo was taken by Edward Sheriff Curtis, a famous American photographer and authority on American Indians. He attempted to document the customs of many American Indian tribes in his 20-volume set, *The North American Indian*, published between 1907 and 1930.

TRIBAL LEADERS

▲ A chief's headdress made by the Tsimshian features a carved face and decorations made of sea lion whiskers, ermine tail, feathers, and abalone shells. Indian chiefs of the Northwest coast wore elaborately carved headdresses for special occasions.

The **tribes** of the Northwest coast and Plateau Indians chose their leaders in different ways.

Born Leaders

Most of the people of the Northwest coast villages could be grouped into four classes. The upper class contained the richest people in the group, with the highest **status**, or rank. This group included chiefs and their relatives. Below the upper class, commoners were people who were not rich, but who did not belong to either of the other two classes that were considered to be lowest—**shamans** (SHAH muhnz) and slaves.

Each village had a head chief who was the highest-ranking member of the most important family. The head chief was also the wealthiest man in the village. He could not gain or keep his status without wealth. The head chief was expected to host great feasts and help poor people, the elderly, and orphans.

Fit to Lead

Among the Plateau Indians, decisions were made by a group who met in a **council**, rather than by a single leader. Each family group had its own spokesperson, or headman. The headman would speak for his group in the council. The headman had no authority over his family group—or the other people in the council. All decisions in the council had to be made by consensus (kuhn SEHN suhs)—that is, most of the people had to agree with the decision.

Plateau peoples generally chose a headman based on his abilities. Usually the best hunter or fisherman was selected. This was not a position that was passed along from father to son. Also, Plateau leadership could shift depending on the task at hand. For example, a salmon chief might direct salmon fishing, and a deer chief would organize the fall hunts.

One leader might take control of an entire tribe in an emergency, such as in times of war. In these cases, a council of headmen would select a war chief. This chief only led during the war. He had no special authority during peacetime.

POSITION OF POWER

The status of a Northwest coast Indian played a part in everything he or she did. For example, social standing determined where a person sat at a feast. It also determined the position of a family's living quarters inside a communal *(kuh MYOO nuhl)* house—a house shared by many people. Chiefs lived at the back of a house, farthest from the entrance. Slaves slept closest to the door or even in the entranceway.

▼ A chief's seat carved by the Kwakiutl in the 1800's. During important ceremonies, a Northwest coast Indian chief sat in such a special seat, which was carved with symbols representing him and his **clan.**

THE ROLES OF MEN AND WOMEN

People of the Northwest coast **cultural** area had different daily chores than those done by people who lived in the Plateau cultural area. Yet, in both regions, there were similarities in the division of the kinds of work done by women and men.

Women's Work

As in most American Indian groups, women of the Plateau and Northwest coast **tribes** were responsible for household chores. In addition to cooking and cleaning, the women made all the baskets and other containers the family would need. They wove the mats and prepared the animal skins that were used for the family's shelter, and they made all of the family's clothing. The women gathered fuel for the fire, as well as the wild plants and fruits that the family ate. Finally, women prepared the food that was provided by the men. Women butchered game animals and prepared the meat for cooking or **preserving**. Fish also had to be cleaned and cooked or thinly sliced and set out to dry.

Men's Work

Men in the Plateau tribes were in charge of those tasks that took place away from the home. Men hunted,

▶ An oil painting, *Salmon Fishing on the Columbia River,* by American artist Ernest Berke, depicts a fishing technique of the Northwest coast and Plateau Indians. Men in these groups sometimes fished by standing on a rocky outcrop above the river rapids and spearing fish from above. If they fell into the rushing river, they were unlikely to survive.

▶ A Tlingit **shaman's** apron
made of deerskin decorated with
painted and beaded designs. In most
Indian groups, women made all of the
clothing, including ceremonial garments.

fished, and made war. When they were at
home, men did chores that furthered their
outside jobs, such as making tools or arrows.

The men of the Northwest coast had many of
the same responsibilities as Plateau men. They
fished, hunted, and went on raiding trips. But
Northwest coast men were also in charge of
woodworking. Men used their woodworking
skills to build canoes and such everyday items
as trays, bowls, cups, and containers. They also
crafted the famous **totem** poles of the Northwest coast and the tribes' ceremonial masks
(see pages 30 and 31).

WORTHY OF RESPECT

Although fish and game were plentiful in the
Plateau cultural area, gathered foods (such as
blackberries, huckleberries, and wild bulbs
and roots) made up a large portion of the
people's diet. Women were responsible for
digging up the roots and bulbs and gathering
the berries. Experts think this might explain,
in part, why women were so highly re-
spected among the Plateau Indians. Women
on the Plateau also owned the house and all
that was in it. A man needed permission
even to take a piece of dried salmon. This
was a source of power for the women, who
had rights equal to those of the men.

SLAVES IN INDIAN SOCIETY

Slavery was common in the Northwest coast **cultural** area. The practice also existed, though much less frequently, among certain **tribes** living in the Plateau cultural area.

The Value of a Life

Slaves were prisoners who were taken from other tribes. Sometimes the slaves came from a tribe that had been defeated in battle. Often, one tribe would raid another specifically to take prisoners to use as slaves. Tribe members did not enslave their own people.

Among the Northwest coast Indians, owning slaves was a sign of wealth. Slaves were considered possessions and had a value equal to a certain number of blankets, shells, or other items. A wealthy man would sometimes give away, set free, or even kill one of his slaves, just to show how rich he was. Getting rid of such a valuable possession was similar to burning money.

▼ A Kwakiutl carved-stone "slave killer" club was decorated with red pigment symbolizing blood. Sacrificing slaves required special **rituals** and weapons, and the purpose of the club may have been more ceremonial than practical.

The Life of a Slave

Slaves performed the same chores as free men and women did in other societies. For example, male slaves of the Northwest coast tribes helped build and paddle the canoes. They fished, hunted, and even took part in raids on other tribes. Female slaves cooked, cleaned, and made clothes and other household items.

Slaves could not take part in a tribe's ceremonies. A slave was also not allowed to marry a free man or woman. Any child born to a slave was also a slave. Worst of all, a slave's life was not his or her own. He or she was the property of another person. Slave owners could kill their slaves for any reason— or no reason at all.

▲ A **totem** pole in Ketchikan, Alaska, made by the Northwest coast Indians shows faces that represent a slave who belonged to the Raven **clan.**

A DEADLY CUSTOM

The Tlingit had a gruesome custom that involved slaves. When a Tlingit chief's house was being built, some of the chief's slaves would be killed. Their bodies were then buried under the corner posts of the house.

Making War

Even peaceful groups of Northwest coast and Plateau Indians sometimes went to war. Although fighting occurred among the Plateau **tribes**, it was more common among the people of the Northwest coast.

Picking a Fight

There were many reasons why people might go to war. In some cases, groups on the Plateau and the Northwest coast went to war specifically to capture slaves.

For the Northwest coast peoples, the other main reason for fighting a war was in response to an insult. In Northwest coast society, people were easily insulted. For example, if someone was given a gift that he or she did not think was valuable enough, he or she considered it an insult.

In a war that was fought in answer to an insult or for revenge, both men and women of the other tribe would be killed. If the war was being fought to capture slaves, however, only adult men of the other tribe were killed. Women, girls, and boys were taken as slaves. The boys would then grow up in captivity and remain slaves.

Ready for Battle

A warrior of the Northwest coast tribes wore a wooden helmet, collar band, a hide vest, and armor carved from cedar. Tlingit armor was made from wooden slats and animal hides. The slats were tied together and wrapped around the warrior's body, over the hide vest. The warriors painted their faces to scare their enemies. Plateau warriors also used a combination of hide and wooden-slat armor.

▼ A Nootka war club, made of wood and stone and decorated with hair and shells. Even fairly simple weapons, such as clubs, were carefully carved and decorated. Some Indians adorned their weapons with the hair of enemies who had been killed in combat.

▲ A Nez Perce warrior on horseback in a photo taken by Edward Sheriff Curtis in the early 1900's. The Nez Perce were considered to be great fighters who carefully planned and executed their battles.

Common weapons used by both groups included spears, knives, bows and arrows, and clubs. Clubs might be made from wood and stone or, in the case of the coastal groups, whalebone.

The coastal groups traveled in canoes to attack their enemies. The warriors usually arrived in the enemy village at night. They waited until dawn to attack, so they could catch their enemies sleeping. Every person in the fleet had a specific job. Some warriors were responsible for watching the canoes during the battle. Other men might be in charge of capturing slaves or setting fire to the enemy houses.

STRONG WORDS

Wars among the Northwest coast groups were not always violent. Sometimes a battle would be fought with words. For example, if one person felt another had insulted him, the two might have a battle of words. If two different groups wanted to fight this way, each could select a leader to speak for the group. Each person would give a speech, talking about the bad things (or consequences) that could happen to his opponent. The person whose threats were considered the most severe won the battle.

THE SPIRIT WORLD

Indians of the Northwest coast and Plateau **cultural** areas believed in a world of powerful spirits. Each group had stories concerning its own spirits.

Indian Legends

Animals played a big role in the **legends** of the Plateau peoples and the Indians of the Northwest coast. Generally, a group's animal spirits were the same as the real animals found in their region. For example, the raven and the whale featured in stories from the Northwest coast, and both animals were common in the Northwest coast area. The coyote, which was frequently found in the Plateau region, was a very powerful force for the Plateau Indians.

Plateau Indians had many stories about how Earth, and everything upon it, came to be. Northwest coast Indians, on the other hand, believed that Earth had always been here. Both groups had stories about how the animal spirits helped humans—by giving people salmon or sunlight, for example.

The people believed that these spirits affected every part of life. If a hunt was unsuccessful, for example, they thought they had done something to make the spirits angry. If a person got sick, it was thought to be the work of the spirits. Indians of the Northwest coast and Plateau worked very hard to keep the spirits pleased. They held ceremonies and dances to give thanks and to ask for help. If a hunt was successful or a sick person recovered, they thought that the spirits had been pleased with their efforts.

▼ A shaman's rattle made by the Haida. Shamans often used such rattles to get in touch with the spirit world. The noise made by the rattle helped the shaman go into a trancelike state in which he or she could communicate with the spirits. The human and animal carvings on this rattle probably show the spirits that the shaman called upon for help.

Medicine People

Indians of the Northwest coast and Plateau believed that the spirit world could be reached with the aid of a religious helper called a **shaman**. Shamans, also called medicine men or medicine women, were important members of Northwest coast and Plateau **tribes**. Because they did not have material wealth, shamans were not among the higher classes of Northwest coast societies. They did have the power to speak to the spirits, however, so they commanded a lot of respect. Shamans were also feared, as it was believed that the power to heal always went with the power to hurt and even kill. Shamans communicated with the spirits to predict the future and to ask for help. Some shamans were also healers. They did not only rely on the spirits to help them cure an illness; they also used the roots, leaves, and flowers of certain plants as medicine.

▲ A Tlingit soul catcher, carved from bone and inlaid with abalone shell. A soul catcher was an important item used by Northwest coast Indian healers. It was believed that some illnesses were caused when the soul left a person's body. In these cases, a shaman was hired to find the soul, catch it in the soul catcher, and return it to the patient.

A TIME TO CELEBRATE

Many ceremonies were held during the winter months because the people thought this was the best time to contact the spirits.

Winter was also the time of year when the people could not find or **preserve** food—so there was less work to do and more free time for such ceremonies. Plateau tribes could also be scattered much of the year but tended to come together in winter.

GUARDIAN SPIRITS

An important belief in the religious systems of the Indians of the Northwest coast and Plateau **cultural** areas was that of the personal **guardian spirit**. This spirit was thought to protect and help a person throughout his or her life.

Vision Quests

Young people were expected to find their guardian spirit when they were in their early teens. Great importance was placed on guardian spirits. Among the Yakima, a person was not considered an adult until he or she found one of these spirits. Many individuals went through an **initiation ceremony** called a **vision quest** to find their guardian spirit.

Before going on a vision quest, a young man first had to purify himself. He might do this by bathing in an icy stream or visiting a **sweat lodge.** The young man then went off alone into the woods or mountains. The vision quest usually involved physical discomfort. The young man could build a fire, but was not allowed to eat. Sometimes he would go without sleep or even stick thorns into himself. Eventually the young man would have a vision of his guardian spirit, though occasionally some failed the quest and were left without a spirit.

Among the Northwest coast **tribes**, girls were not allowed to go off alone because their parents worried that they would be kidnapped. Instead, a guardian spirit had to come to a girl as she went about her daily routine at home.

◀ Ornaments of bone hang from this Tlingit **shaman's** necklace. The face carved into the large pendant represents the shaman's guardian spirit.

SWEAT LODGES

Small sweat lodges were often made of mud and covered with mats and tree branches. Larger sweat lodges might be made of logs. In one kind of sweat lodge, the entrance was sealed from the outside and then someone inside poured water over hot rocks that had been placed on the floor. This created steam, which caused the people in the sweat lodge to perspire. Sweat lodge ceremonies were designed to purify the body, cure illnesses, and influence spirits. Most sweat lodges were built near rivers so the people using them could jump into the cool water after leaving the lodge.

Dancing Societies

Indians of the Northwest coast had societies that performed dances during special winter ceremonies. They wore beautifully carved masks that represented their guardian spirits. The Kwakiutl on the Northwest coast were noted for their especially elaborate ceremonies.

▼ A large sweat lodge in the style of Northwest coast Indians in British Columbia.

POTLATCH CEREMONIES

Potlatches *(POT lach ez)* were ceremonial feasts that lasted several days. The host of the feast, a person of wealth, would give gifts to the guests. The ceremonies were especially important among the Northwest coast Indians.

Reasons to Celebrate

Potlatches were held to celebrate major events. The ceremony could be held to mark a birth, a child's passage into adulthood, a marriage, or even a death. The Indians of the northern Plateau were the only Plateau Indians to hold potlatches.

During a Plateau Indian potlatch, the host gave dried or smoked deer meat to all of his guests. The potlatches hosted by Northwest coast Indians were very different. These ceremonies were meant to display the host's wealth and increase his standing in the community.

◀ A Tlingit robe that would have been worn only to a ceremonial event, such as a potlatch. The robe, made of mountain goat wool and otter fur, has an overall design that represents the brown bear **totem.**

Quite a Party

The word *potlatch* comes from a Chinook word meaning "to give away." The host of a potlatch gave away many valuable items to his guests. These gifts could include blankets, masks, furs, shells, robes, tools, and sheets of copper. Gifts might even include ownership of certain berry-picking areas or the right to sing certain songs. As each gift was handed out, its value was announced.

The more gifts a host gave away—and the more valuable the gifts—the wealthier the host appeared. For certain groups, potlatches were, therefore, highly competitive. Each host wanted to appear wealthier than the last.

For a large potlatch, a host might invite people from many **tribes**. Feeding all of these people and providing them with gifts would have been very expensive and time consuming. The host had to begin preparing for the feast months in advance. Only the richest people could afford to host a large potlatch. Singing and dancing were also important parts of a potlatch. Both the songs and dances told stories about the host's family.

SHIFTING WEALTH

For some Indian cultures, the potlatch was a means of showing and gaining **status** for a host. In a culture that held potlatches, people gained status not by how much they had, but by how much they gave away. For other Indian cultures, the potlatch was not as much about status. Instead, it was a means of distributing wealth from the richer to the poorer members of a group.

▶ A spoon, thought to have been made by either the Haida or Tlingit, carved from the horn of a mountain goat. The spoon features the images of a raven and a human on the handle. Such a spoon would have been used during a potlatch feast. It would then have been given away to a guest at the end of the potlatch.

FOOD CEREMONIES

▲ *Bear Dance, Preparing for a Bear Hunt,* an engraving based on an oil painting (dating from the 1800's) by the American artist George Catlin.

I n addition to the **potlatch**, the Indians of the Northwest coast and Plateau **cultural** areas held other ceremonies that centered on food. They had **rituals** to help find food, and they had celebrations to give thanks for food.

Praying for Plenty

Indians of the Plateau held ceremonies to ask the spirits to help them find food. The Winter Dance of the Nez Perce was one of these ceremonies. During the feast, the people sang songs and performers acted out the process of hunting or gathering foods. These dances and songs were the people's way of telling the spirits what they needed.

GIVING SOMETHING BACK

Plateau groups believed that any time they took something from the Earth, they needed to put something back. Even the smallest root or plant they gathered was accounted for. They would bury a gift, such as a bead, to show their thanks for the item they had gathered from the Earth.

Northwest coast Indians often held a bear dance before a bear hunt. As part of the bear dance, performers acted like bears and wore bear costumes. Through this dance, the people were asking the spirit of the bear to provide food for their hunters.

The people of the Northwest coast and Plateau **tribes** also made sure to say a prayer before and after killing an animal. They believed this honored the spirit of the animal. If they forgot to honor the animal spirit, they worried that it would no longer allow living animals of its kind to be caught.

Giving Thanks

Indians of the Northwest coast and Plateau cultural areas all had thanksgiving rituals known as First Food Ceremonies. After eating the first salmon caught in a given year, the Plateau Indians would throw its bones into the water where the fish was caught. They believed that this would ensure more salmon in the future. The Northwest coast Indians also followed this ritual. For their ceremony, though, the people made sure that the fish's skeleton was undamaged. They feared that if even one bone were missing when the salmon went to be reborn under the sea, the fish would be deformed when it returned.

Tribes had similar rituals to give thanks for other animals they hunted and also for the plants that they gathered. In the spring, the Cayuse, Umatilla, and Walla Walla tribes all held a Root Feast to honor the plants that were so important to their survival.

▼ Indians on the Flathead **Reservation** *(rehz uhr VAY shuhn)* in Montana perform a traditional ceremonial dance in a photo taken by an unknown photographer in 1921.

WEDDINGS AND FUNERALS

Northwest coast and Plateau Indians had special **rituals** for weddings. Ceremonies to honor the dead were also important.

Finding a Partner

Some Plateau Indian weddings took place at a dance. As a man came to face the woman he wanted to marry, he placed a stick on her shoulder and danced next to her. If the woman did not want to marry the man, she simply knocked the stick off her shoulder. If the woman allowed the man to dance with her and left the stick on her shoulder until the dance was over, the two were married.

For the Northwest coast **tribes**, marriages were arranged. First, the groom's family would talk to the family of a possible bride. Then they would hold a feast. Finally, the groom's family presented gifts to the girl's family. These gifts were known as the **bride price**. If the family accepted the gifts, the couple would be married. There was no further ceremony needed.

▼ A Kwakiutl wedding ceremony staged by photographer Edward Sheriff Curtis in 1914 during the filming of a movie about the tribe.

Final Farewell

After a Plateau Indian died, his or her body was bathed. The person's face was painted, and he or she was dressed in new clothes and wrapped in a mat. The person might be given a **rockslide burial** or be buried near the river with his or her head pointing downstream. For a rockslide burial, the body would be placed on a slope. The other members of the tribe would then push rocks down the slope to cover the body.

Some Northwest coast tribes, such as the Haida, Tlingit, and Tsimshian, cremated, or burned, their dead. Other Northwest tribes, including the southern Kwakiutl and the Nootka, practiced **tree burials**. Among these tribes, the dead person's body was placed in a wooden box. The box was then hung in a tree far from the village.

◀ A statue carved of wood by the Kwakiutl. Experts believe this statue would have been used to decorate the box into which a Kwakiutl chief's body was placed for burial. The eagle on the figure's head may represent the chief's **clan.**

GONE FOREVER

Among the Yakima, a dead person's house was burned or taken apart after his or her burial. This was to prevent other people from feeling sad whenever they passed the house. Some Northwest coast tribes also burned down a house after the owner died, in order to keep the person's spirit from haunting the family.

EVERYDAY WORKS OF ART

Wood, plants, and animal skins were all used by Northwest coast and Plateau Indians to create containers of all kinds. These beautifully crafted pieces were also valuable trade items.

Beautiful Baskets

People from the Northwest coast and Plateau **cultural** areas used such plant fibers as grasses or the bark from cedar trees to make baskets and bags. They wove into the work zigzag patterns and such shapes as triangles and squares. The people also used dyes to decorate the plant fibers.

Plateau Indians made flat bags, which they used to carry their possessions. They crafted circular baskets for carrying plants, roots, and fruits. The baskets often included a cord that allowed a woman to carry the basket around her chest or forehead. This left her hands free for gathering.

◀ A Tlingit basket made from spruce root features an image of a killer whale.

SIGNING HER WORK

Every woman had her own unique style of basket weaving. According to historians, certain patterns and the placement of those patterns act as a signature of the woman who wove the basket.

Northwest coast Indians also created a variety of baskets. Clam baskets were loosely woven so that water and mud could pass through the openings. Cooking baskets, on the other hand, were tightly woven so that water would not leak out.

Amazing Boxes

In addition to baskets, Indians of the Northwest coast used wooden boxes for everything from storage to cooking to burying their dead. To make a box, a woodworker took a long rectangular board and made three grooves in it. Then he used steam to soften the wood. When the wood was soft enough, the woodworker bent the wood at the grooves, making a square or rectangle. The spot where the two ends of the board met was joined together with tiny wooden pegs or laces. A grooved piece of wood was then fitted into the sides to make the bottom of the box. The pieces fit together so well that many boxes could actually hold water without leaking. The wooden boxes were then decorated with carvings of animals and other designs.

▼ A Tlingit box, one of four that were used for a **shaman's** burial. The cedar boxes contained the man's bones and the tools of his trade, which included masks as well as dolls with broken arms and other ailments.

Indian Carvings

▲ A totem pole, called "Hole-in-the-Sky," which was originally used as a ceremonial entrance to a Tsimshian house. The pole features a combination of ancestor figures and totem animals, including the wolf, which was the pole owner's principal totem.

The Indians of the Northwest coast **cultural** area are famous for their beautiful carvings. The people of these groups made **totem** poles and masks out of wood.

Faces in Wood

Masks were not meant to be works of art but had special ceremonial purposes. They were used in dances and **rituals** and were meant to represent such figures as animal spirits.

The masks were carved of cedar wood and often contained two or three faces in one. During a performance, the person wearing the mask would pull a cord to reveal a second mask (or third) under the first. Since the person was performing at night, with only the light of a fire, this was an amazing effect. People watching did not see the performer pulling a cord; they only saw what looked like another mask magically appearing from nowhere.

Totem Poles

The **tribes** of the Northwest coast are probably best known for the amazing carved columns known as totem poles, which were more than decorative items. Each one, carved of cedar wood, tells a story. Often, the symbols on a totem pole represent the family history of the person to

TOTEMS

A totem is a symbol for a tribe, **clan**, or family. A clan totem may be a bird, fish, animal, plant, or other natural object. Clan members are often known by the name of the clan's totem.

Totem poles can include carvings that represent both the totems and the ancestors of a family or clan. These carvings are stacked one on another, in various combinations. There is a common belief that the lower a carving appears on a totem pole, the less important it is. That is not true. It is impossible to judge the importance of a carving by where it appears on a pole.

whom the pole belongs. There are many kinds of totem poles. House frontal poles are tall and are placed against the front of a house. Sometimes they serve as a doorway, with a hole carved in the bottom of the pole for an entrance. Other house posts include interior posts that support the roof.

Freestanding poles include large welcome posts, memorial posts that were used to honor chiefs that have passed away, and **mortuary** *(MAWR chu EHR ee)* poles. Some tribes used mortuary poles, which have a small recess on top, to hold the coffins of important tribe members.

There is a long tradition of pole carving in the Northwest coast. But, since wood quickly rots in the humid Pacific Northwest region, few totem poles that were made before 1800 exist today. Stories told by the Haida and Tlingit tribes, however, show that they were probably carving totem poles long before that time.

▶ A transformation mask was actually two or more masks in one. In this Haida mask, a carving of a thunderbird, shown open, reveals a human face inside. This was meant to show the dual animal/human nature of spirits.

PICTURES IN STONE

Pictograms are painted images found on rocks. **Petroglyphs** are images that are chipped or chiseled into the rocks. The peoples in the Northwest coast and Plateau regions created many works of art on the rocks near their homes.

Coastal Art

Many of the pictograms created by peoples of the Northwest coast have been found on the shores of rivers and lakes. Petroglyphs in this region, on the other hand, are usually found on rocks facing the ocean.

Although different groups created different pictures, there are common themes in the rock art. Most art contains both human figures and animals. However, the pictures rarely look realistic. For example, some rock art features men that have bent arms and legs that make them look a little like frogs.

DATING THE ART

Archaeologists have a hard time dating rock art. Often, scientists use **radiocarbon dating** to determine an item's age. All living things contain radiocarbon, a kind of carbon that plants absorb from the air and that people and animals take in by eating plants. After a living thing dies, the radiocarbon breaks down at a set rate. By measuring how much radiocarbon remains in an object, scientists can determine when the living thing died. Unfortunately, because rock is not a living thing, radiocarbon dating does not help scientists determine a date for rock art. On the Northwest coast, scientists found a petroglyph below a 1,000-year-old tree, so they know that piece of art is at least 1,000 years old.

◀ This large boulder, called the Wallula (*wah LOO lah*) stone, is covered in petroglyphs created by Indians living on the Columbia Plateau. The stone was removed from the Columbia River during a dam-building project and moved to the Umatilla Indian **Reservation.**

Much of the rock art of the Northwest coast region includes images of the animals that were important in the lives and **legends** of the people. These include sea mammals, birds, wolves, bears, mountain goats, and salmon. Many of the pictograms and petroglyphs seem to recount some of the people's legends. Canoes and other items made by people also feature in the art.

▲ Petroglyphs carved by the Nootka featuring fish and other marine life. Of great importance to the Northwest coast Indians, salmon and sea mammals are frequently depicted in their petroglyphs.

Art of the Plateau

The rock art of the Plateau region is mostly found on the canyons and boulders scattered throughout the region. Although the different regions had different artistic styles, there are some similarities.

Human figures appear in the pictures, as do spirit beings. The animals featured in the rock art of the Plateau region represent the many animals found there, including birds, coyotes, and deer. Experts believe that, as in the case of the Northwest coast art, these animals probably had a spiritual significance.

TRADITIONAL UPBRINGING

A merican Indian life was marked by tradition. From the time a person was born until he or she died, there were **rituals** to celebrate each new stage of life.

In the Beginning

Women in Northwest coast and Plateau societies gave birth in special lodges away from the rest of the village. In the Northwest coast **cultural** area, the mother and baby spent the first four days of the child's life alone in the lodge. Often, the baby wore a tight-fitting cap made of shredded bark that narrowed and elongated his or her soft skull.

▼ A mask carved of wood, depicting a Tlingit woman with a labret. The labret looks like a plug and goes into a hole below the lower lip. As shown on this mask in lighter wood, the labret sticks out above and below the lower lip. A woman could increase the size of her labret over time by gradually stretching the hole in her lip.

Mothers strapped their babies to cradleboards and carried them everywhere they went. In the Plateau region, a mother strapped the cradleboard to her back so that her hands were free for work. Among the Northwest coast Indians, mothers freed up their hands by hanging the cradleboard from a roof beam in the house.

At the age of 1, a Plateau baby was given his or her name during a naming ceremony. Babies from the Northwest coast were named after an ancestor at birth. Later, the child might be given another name at a **potlatch**.

READY TO GET MARRIED

Among wealthy families of the Haida, Tlingit, and Tsimshian, a girl received her first **labret** (LAY breht)—lip ornament—when she entered into womanhood by the standards of her people. In these tribes, the labret was used to show that a girl was ready to be married.

Entering Adulthood

The point at which a child entered adulthood varied from **tribe** to tribe. Among some Plateau tribes, a boy typically went on a **vision quest** before entering **puberty**—some time between the ages of 8 and 12 years old. He might not be considered a man, however, until he had reached puberty. In some tribes of the Northwest coast, such as the Tlingits, a boy was sent to the home of his mother's brother when he was 8 years old. That is when he first began to learn his adult responsibilities. He was not considered a man, however, until he had killed his first game animal.

Girls in Plateau and Northwest coast societies were generally considered adults when they reached puberty. This usually occurred around the age of 13. At this stage, a Plateau Indian girl went to a separate lodge and had her hair bound up in rolls. She wore plain clothing and painted her face either yellow or red. The young woman purified herself in a **sweat lodge** before returning to the village.

Among some Northwest coast tribes, a girl had to spend a few weeks in a dark hideaway, where her grandmother looked after her. During this time, the young woman went without food for a few days. The hunger may have made a girl more susceptible to making contact with a **guardian spirit.**

▶ A cedar carving depicts a Kwakiutl Indian whose head had been shaped. Some Indian groups used hard cradleboards instead of tight bark caps to shape a baby's head. By the 1900's, head shaping had died out among the tribes of the Northwest coast and Plateau. The last known person with a shaped head died in the 1920's.

INDIAN VILLAGES

The Indians of the Northwest coast and Plateau **cultural** areas had different villages for the summer and winter months. This allowed them to be close to food sources when the weather was right for hunting, fishing, or gathering plants.

Moving with the Seasons

During the spring and summer months, people spent almost all of their time outside. This was the time of year for fishing, hunting, and gathering the plants that were blooming across the countryside. During the day, the people did their chores outside. These chores included preparing food for winter storage and making crafts and tools. They only used their houses for sleeping and for shelter if the weather turned bad.

During these warm months, Plateau Indians lived in houses that were easy to put together, take apart, and move from place to place. Each family had a temporary shelter in which they lived. Several families would camp together to form a summer village. Villages might be set up near a stream during the first **salmon run** of the spring, and

WHO LIVES HERE?
The winter homes of the Northwest coast Indians who lived farthest north were decorated on the outside with carvings or paintings. People could tell which **clan** the family belonged to just by looking at the designs. The carvings and paintings also detailed the family's history.

▶ A traditional Plateau Indian dwelling, photographed by Edward Sheriff Curtis in 1910, is made of wooden poles covered with reed mats. Such dwellings offered protection from sun, rain, and wind and could be easily taken apart and moved to a new summer village.

then moved to a meadow when certain fruits were ripe. In addition to individual family shelters, summer villages might include large shared lodges. These structures allowed a group of related families, called a **band**, to live together.

In the winter, the Plateau Indians moved to more permanent dwellings called pit houses (see page 39). Like summer villages, winter villages contained large communal longhouses, which could be used for winter ceremonies, as well as for living space.

Most Indians of the Northwest coast also divided their time between two villages. In the summer, they set up simple structures, usually on the banks of rivers. Their winter villages were usually located in more sheltered areas, close to the beach. The huge wooden longhouses, in which extended families lived together, all faced out to sea.

▼ A water color by John Webber depicts a Nootka village off the west coast of present-day Vancouver Island. Webber painted the work in 1778 while on a voyage with British explorer James Cook. The houses of Northwest coast Indians were often placed close to the water's edge because the people obtained much of their food from the sea and did most of their traveling by boat.

HOMES FOR ALL SEASONS

Northwest coast and Plateau Indians used the materials that were common in their territories to build houses.

Summer Homes

Plateau Indians made summer shelters that were shaped like tents or tipis, often made of wooden poles covered with woven mats. The Indians of the Northwest coast built their temporary shelters out of brush or bark.

A different type of structure, known as a longhouse, was also used in summer. A longhouse had a frame made from wooden poles that were arched to meet in the center. The poles were covered with grasses and reeds (tall grasses with hollow, jointed stalks). Summer longhouses could be more than 60 feet (18 meters) long and 15 feet (4.5 meters) wide.

▲ A 1784 engraving of a work painted by John Webber shows the inside of a Nootka house. At the ceiling, strips of fish hang from the rafters, causing the fish to be **preserved** with the smoke from the fire.

BEST OF BOTH WORLDS

Like other Northwest coast Indians, the Chinook built rectangular houses out of cedar wood. But they placed their longhouses partially underground over pits—a technique that was more common in the Plateau **cultural** area.

Winter Lodgings

In the winter, Plateau Indians lived in pit houses. A pit house was made of wooden posts that were set up over a large, circular hole in the ground. The posts were covered with mats made of grasses and reeds and, sometimes, a layer of earth. A hole in the roof was used for a smoke hole and to exit and enter the dwelling.

The winter longhouse was built of posts that were covered with water-repellent mats. To further waterproof the house, the builders lined the inside walls with animal skins.

Northwest coast Indians used redcedar trees to build longhouses that were shared by extended families or **clans**. The house was built with four corner posts—large tree trunks that were set into deep holes in the ground. The walls were made of cedar planks. The roof was made of cedar planks and pieces of bark that overlapped and were held down with rocks. There were no windows in the longhouse, and there was only a small opening for an entrance. A small opening in the roof allowed smoke from inside to escape.

Many families shared a winter longhouse, which could measure up to 150 feet (46 meters) long and 60 feet (18 meters) wide. Each family had its own living space, which was separated from the others by mats. Each space opened to the center of the house.

▼ A pit house, such as this one from British Columbia, was the kind of house in which Plateau Indians lived during winter.

CLOTHING AND JEWELRY

Most Indians of the Northwest coast and Plateau **cultural** areas wore very little clothing. Instead, they decorated themselves with jewelry and body paints.

Casual Wear

For the people of the Northwest coast, everyday clothing was chosen for its usefulness. When the weather was cold, a man's main piece of clothing was a blanket made of cedar bark. A woman usually wore a skirt made of grass or shredded bark that was attached to a cord and tied around the waist. A blanket made of cedar bark covered the woman from her shoulders to the top of her feet. Cedar was plentiful in the area, and the bark protected the wearer from wind and rain. People did not use the rough outside bark for clothing but rather used the soft bark underneath the outer bark. People also made yarn from the fur of mountain goats.

Clothing was simple among the Plateau Indians. In the summer, a man usually wore a **breechcloth**. A breechcloth is a narrow band of cloth made of animal skin that is passed between the legs and looped over the front and rear of a belt. Women wore aprons that were made of animal hides or woven plant fibers. During cold weather, the people added leg wrappings and capes or robes. Rabbit fur was a favorite material for making warm winter robes and blankets.

▲ A hat woven by the Haida people from spruce roots.

Body Art

Only women from certain Northwest coast **tribes** wore lip ornaments, called **labrets**. Both sexes from all of the Northwest coast and Plateau tribes sometimes wore ornaments in their ears and noses, though. These ornaments were made from bone, wood, copper, fur, or shells.

Tattooing was also common among the Northwest coast tribes. To create a tattoo, a person used a thorn or a sharpened bone to poke holes in the skin. Then charcoal was rubbed into the holes. The people also painted their bodies and faces.

CHILKAT BLANKETS

Although many tribes made blankets, none were as famous for the craft as the Chilkat *(CHIHL kat)*. The Chilkat were members of the Tlingit group of Indians. They lived in southeastern Alaska.

The Chilkat made blankets from mountain goat wool and cedar bark. The blankets featured beautiful designs and had a fringe along the bottom and sides. Chilkat blankets were a sign of wealth among the Northwest coast Indians and were only worn on special occasions by the highest-ranking people in a village.

▼ A Chilkat blanket decorated with killer whale designs. To make their famous blankets, Chilkat men painted a design on a wooden board. The women then copied the design when they wove the blankets. Chilkat blankets were used as dancing costumes and shawls, but were also a form of money.

FISHING FOR A MEAL

Fish, especially salmon, were the lifeblood of the Northwest coast and Plateau Indians. Annual **salmon runs** helped ensure that the people had enough to eat.

Food for Today

Every spring and summer, salmon leave the Pacific Ocean and travel up rivers and streams to lay their eggs. The people of the Northwest coast and Plateau **cultural** areas spent much of this time of the year catching salmon and **preserving** it—that is, preparing the salmon to keep it from spoiling. Both groups used similar methods to fish for salmon.

One method used by the Northwest coast Indians was to wait for the fish near rapids. As the salmon jumped through the air to clear the rapids, the fishermen killed them with spears or caught them in baskets. Some Plateau Indians, such as the Nez Perce, built towers at certain spots on the river. They placed **weirs** (*wihrz*) in the water beneath the towers to slow the fish down so they could spear them. Northwest coast Indians used weirs, as well. Both groups also used nets to

◀ Yakima fishermen demonstrate the tribe's technique for catching fish in a 1940's photograph. The men had built a platform near Celio Falls on the Columbia River, from which they caught fish in long-handled nets.

▶ This Tlingit fishhook is made of cedar and cork, and it was carved to look like a man holding a float over his head. The actual hook, shown behind the carved figure, had an iron point. Such hooks were for catching halibut and were designed to catch fish no larger than could be safely hauled into a canoe. The Tlingit started to use iron fishhooks after contact with Europeans in the 1700's.

catch fish. The Plateau Indians sometimes stood on platforms, leaning over to scoop up the salmon. To prevent accidents, a fisherman would often tie a rope around his waist and secure it to something on land.

Northwest coast Indians also fished for eulachon *(YOO luh kon),* flounder, halibut, herring, sardine, and sturgeon *(STUR juhn).* These Indians also gathered such shellfish as clams, mussels, and oysters. In addition to salmon, Plateau Indians caught sturgeon, trout, and whitefish.

Saving the Leftovers

When the men returned from fishing, the women cleaned the catch. Indians ate some fish fresh, but most of the catch was prepared for storage. To preserve clams, the women from the coastal **tribes** would remove the meat from the shells and string it on sticks. They then smoked the clams over a fire. They often smoked salmon to preserve it, as well. Both the Northwest coast and Plateau Indians cut the fish into strips, which were hung on racks. The fish would either be smoked over a fire or allowed to dry in the sun.

FISH HUNTING

Plateau Indians also fished using a bow and arrow. The fishermen would stand on the banks of a river, or on a platform, and shoot at the fish in the water. The arrows had strings attached, so the fisherman could pull a fish in after shooting it.

HUNTING AND GATHERING

▲ Camas lilies carpet the Weippe *(WEE ipe)* Prairie in present-day northern Idaho, which is part of the Nez Perce National Historical Park.

The peoples of the Northwest coast and Plateau **cultural** areas did not live on fish alone. Both groups added to their diets by hunting game and gathering plants for food.

On the Hunt

Indians on the coast hunted sea lions, sea otters, and seals using **harpoons** *(hahr POONZ)* and wooden clubs. Whales were important to Indians of the Northwest coast, but people did not often hunt them. Most **tribes** just waited for a dead whale to wash up on the shore.

The Nootka, however, were famous whalers of the region. A Nootka whaling team used a special canoe that was about 30 feet (9 meters) long and could hold eight men. The whalers used harpoons to kill their prey, so they had to get very close to the whale.

Some coastal tribes also hunted on land. Their prey included bear, deer, elk, mountain goat, and even moose. Plateau Indians also hunted bear, deer, and elk. Sometimes the hunters would cover themselves in the hides or antlers of their prey. When they got close enough, they killed the animal using a bow and arrow. Plateau Indians also caught rabbits, squirrels, and water birds. To catch a duck, a hunter might place a large, hollowed-out gourd over his head. Then he would wade into the water until just the gourd was showing on the surface. When he got close enough to a duck, the hunter grabbed the bird's feet.

Gathering Nature's Bounty

Camas *(CAM uhs)*, a lily bulb, was a favorite of the Northwest coast and Plateau peoples. The women used digging sticks of sharpened willow to gather the bulbs in late June and July. Camas could be eaten raw or roasted over a fire. To store extra camas, Plateau women steamed the bulbs and ground them into cakes. Women of the coast dried their extra bulbs.

The women also gathered blackberries, huckleberries, and strawberries. Whatever fruit was not eaten fresh was made into cakes by the Plateau women and stored for the winter. Women of the coast **preserved** berries by drying them and storing them in oil.

A DANGEROUS MOVE

Sometimes a hunter would jump on a whale after it had been harpooned and stab it with his knife. If the whaler could stay on the whale while it went under water and then came back up, he was considered a hero.

▲ An engraving provides an unrealistic view of how Indians, such as the Nootka, hunted whales. Made in the 1500's by Johann Gottfried *(GOT freed)*, the engraving is based on accounts from the priest and explorer Jose de Acosta *(hoh zaih duh KAWST uh)*. In the engraving, a lone man seems to be hunting a whale, but actually a team was used. Some men were in charge of paddling the boat, another steered, and the chief acted as harpooner.

MEALTIMES

Similar methods of food preparation were used by the Indians of the Northwest coast and Plateau **cultural** areas. For the coastal people, the mealtime ritual was more complicated than the preparation of the food.

Cooking Styles

Food was often roasted over a fire, but hot stones were also used for cooking. A woman would heat stones in a fire and then use wooden sticks to pick them up. After dipping the stones in water to remove any ashes, the cook would transfer them to a container that was partially filled with water. This container could be a basket, box, or hollowed-out log. The hot rocks would cause the water to boil. A basket of raw food was placed in the container with the boiling water, and more hot stones were added.

Women also used stones to bake food in a roasting pit. For a roasting pit, a shallow hole was lined with large pebbles. A fire was built on top of the pebbles. Once the rocks were hot, the fire was smothered. Food was wrapped in leaves and placed in the pit.

▼ A wooden Haida dish carved in the shape of a canoe. The dish would have been used to serve such foods as dried fruits moistened with fish oil.

Sharing a Meal

A mealtime among the Northwest coast **tribes** was a formal affair. Before sitting down, everyone rinsed his or her mouth out with water. A towel made of shredded cedar bark was then passed around. After wiping his or her hands once, each person dipped them in a finger bowl of water and wiped them again. At this point, everyone at the table took a sip of water from the drinking bowl. It was not considered proper to drink during the meal. If a person needed to drink during the meal, people would think he or she had eaten too much.

People served food on wooden platters shaped like flat-bottomed canoes. They ate with spoons that had been carved from wood or mountain goat horns. Sometimes they used clamshells as eating utensils. After eating, the people used a wooden finger bowl to clean their hands and dried them with the cedar-bark towel. After the last person dried his or her hands, the drinking bowl was passed around the table again.

▶ A Salish spoon made of bison horn, with a double handle carved to resemble birds' heads. Such items were often brought by guests to ceremonial events.

TABLE MANNERS
As they ate, the Northwest coast peoples sipped food from the tips of spoons. It was not polite for someone to open his or her mouth wide enough to expose the teeth while eating.

LIFE LESSONS

Children from the Northwest coast and Plateau **tribes** did not go to school. They learned by following the example of others in their group. Stories told by elders also served to teach the young.

Following the Leader

Boys and girls were taught separately among both the Northwest coast Indians and the people of the Plateau **cultural** area. The men of the tribe taught boys how to fish, hunt, and make weapons. Girls learned how to do the work that would one day be expected of them from the older women in the tribe.

In **matrilineal** societies, such as the Haida, Tlingit, and Tsimshian of the Northwest coast, a boy was taught by his mother's brother, and not by his father. The child left his parents' household when he was still young to go live with his uncle.

▼ Coast Salish Indians dressed in traditional clothes and head-dresses. They carry the same kinds of weapons used by their ancestors.

Children got a lot of special attention when they mastered their new skills. Among the Plateau peoples, a tribe's best hunter would eat a boy's first kill or catch of fish. The highest-ranking woman would eat the first plant foods collected by a girl. Giving away their "first foods" in this way also taught the children to be generous.

Listen and Learn

Storytelling was an important part of life in the Plateau and the Northwest coast cultural areas—whether the story was acted out during a **potlatch** or told around a fire on a cold winter night. The stories were handed down through the years from generation to generation. Not just meant to entertain, these tales taught the young people about their tribe's customs and beliefs. Tribal elders and grandparents were the main storytellers among Plateau Indian groups. They watched the children while their parents were away hunting, fishing, and gathering food.

▼ A Cayuse mother and her child in a photograph taken in 1910. An Indian mother spent nearly every waking moment with her infant. By carrying her baby in a cradleboard, she had her hands free for work while her baby was kept safe.

HOW THE SUN AND STARS CAME TO BE

Indian children learned many things from the stories they were told. Some stories taught children about the society they lived in and its customs. Other stories gave children an explanation for how the world came to be or why things happened in certain ways. This Tsimshian **legend,** for example, explains the sun and stars.

"Before anything in the world was created, there was only the chief in the sky and his people. One of the chief's sons was named The-One-Who-Walks-All-Over-the-Sky. The dark, empty sky made The-One-Who-Walks-All-Over-the-Sky sad, so one day he made a mask, put it on, and lit it on fire. Then he ran through the sky from east to west. That is why the sun travels from east to west during the day. When he slept, sparks flew out of The-One-Who-Walks-All-Over-the-Sky's mouth, becoming the stars. When he felt very happy, The-One-Who-Walks-All-Over-the-Sky would paint his face with red ocher [pigment]."

TRANSPORTATION

I ndians of the Northwest coast and Plateau **cultural** areas traveled on local waterways. The **tribes** used different kinds of canoes.

Seafaring Boats

Every man in the Northwest coast tribes knew how to build small family canoes that were used on rivers and streams. But only expert craftsmen built the larger, ocean-going canoes. The Haida, Nootka, and Tlingit were the main groups that built such large canoes. The Haida canoes were the largest, at more than 60 feet (18 meters) long. They used these large canoes to make ocean voyages.

The Indians of the Northwest coast used a redcedar tree to build their canoes. If the canoe makers could not find a fallen tree, they cut one down using hammers and sharp stone chisels. They then removed the branches and bark and built a fire along the center of the log. As the wood burned, the canoe maker chipped away the charred pieces until the center of the tree was hollow. Next, the canoe maker poured water into the hollowed-out log and added hot stones to boil the water. The boiling water caused the wood to soften. This allowed the canoe maker to insert wooden boards, called spreaders, across the center of the log to widen it. The canoe spreaders were later used as seats. The canoe maker then emptied out the water and sanded the canoe with the rough skin of a dogfish—a kind of small shark. Finally, the canoe maker painted the canoe and gave it a coating of whale oil.

▼ A model of a Tlingit canoe, decorated with an eye design on the prow (front) and stern (back). Northwest coast Indians carved and painted their canoes, and sometimes their paddles as well. The designs might represent the boat owner's **totem** animals or spirits that could protect the sailors.

River Craft

Each tribe among the Plateau Indians had its own style of boat. The Okanagan, Shuswap, Kutenai, and Thompson Indians used canoes that were made of bark. The Flathead made their canoes by hollowing logs out with fire, as did the tribes of the Northwest coast. The Coeur d'Alene used rafts that were made of mats. These were the same mats the people used to cover their lodgings. In the case of the rafts, though, the mats were rolled up, bound together, and shaped into a point in front and back.

▼ Kutenai Indians with a canoe, photographed by Edward Sheriff Curtis in 1910. To make a canoe, the Kutenai first built a framework of long wooden poles crossed with cedar ribs. Then they covered the outside of the canoe with a large piece of white pine bark, which was trimmed to fit. Holes punched along the edges of the cover allowed the bark to be lashed to the canoe frame. Long wooden poles were attached along the top edges of the canoe, and a spreader bar was placed across the center.

OTHER MEANS OF TRANSPORTATION

The people of the Plateau cultural area could not always use canoes for transportation. Often, they needed to move across the land on foot. Before horses were introduced to North America by the Spanish, the Plateau Indians used dogs to help carry their loads. In fact, many American Indian groups used dogs as work animals.

TRADING AMONG TRIBES

The different **tribes** in the Northwest coast **cultural** area traded extensively among themselves, as did the tribes on the Plateau. With the Chinook acting as middlemen, these two culture groups were also able to trade with each other.

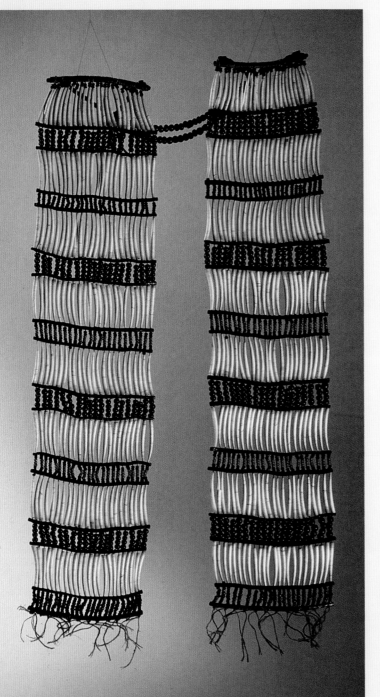

Valuable Goods

Although tribes in the Northwest coast region lived in similar environments, they still found reasons to trade with one another. For example, the Nootka—the only whale hunters in the area—often supplied whale oil and bones to other tribes. Many tribes along the coast also traded for Haida canoes and Chilkat blankets. The blankets were prized for their beauty but were also used as a form of money, as were other kinds of blankets. The Indians also used dentalium *(dehn TAY lee uhm)* shells as currency. Indians mostly found these tooth-shaped shells off present-day Vancouver Island in Nootka territory. Other tribes obtained dentalium through trade with the Nootka.

◀ Nootka hair ornaments made of tusk shells and glass beads. When a Nootka girl of high **status** reached a certain age, she wore such ornaments in her hair. When the time came for the girl to marry, she removed the ornaments, and a **potlatch** was held to mark the occasion of her coming of age. The ornaments were also valuable trade items.

TRADE TALK
The Chinook were expert traders. They even developed a special language, a mix of local languages, which they used to communicate with the rest of the tribes. This language was different from their traditional language, which members of the tribe spoke among themselves.

Sharing the Wealth

The Plateau groups used shells for money, to decorate their clothing, and in jewelry. These tribes had no way to get seashells other than from the coastal groups. Chinook traders brought shells and other coastal items to the Plateau region. In return, they brought back items that the coastal tribes desired. For example, the Nez Perce people were famous for the bags they made. One kind was made of woven grasses and was decorated with geometric patterns. Another kind was a long flat bag made out of cornhusks. The Nez Perce got the cornhusks in trade with Indians from the Plains.

Tribes on the Columbia Plateau also met at annual trade fairs to exchange goods. The largest meeting place was at a spot now called The Dalles *(dalz)*, on the lower Columbia River in present-day Oregon. Tribes from all over the region met at The Dalles, as did some Plains Indians, peoples from the Northwest coast, and California Indians.

▼ Trade fairs offered Indians of the Northwest coast and Plateau regions a chance to obtain vital goods. These fairs also served an important social function. Members of different tribes who ordinarily had no contact were able to meet and mingle during trade fairs. In fact, it was not uncommon for friendships to start at trade fairs that led to marriage.

SPORTS AND GAMES

Games have always been important in American Indian culture. Some games were meant for fun. Others taught important skills. Many of these games involved forms of betting.

Guessing Games

People of the Northwest coast and Plateau regions played several guessing games. Often, the players bet on the outcome. **Wagers** could include baskets, blankets, or other items of value.

In a guessing game played among Indians of the Northwest coast **cultural** area, a player took a small stone and passed it from one hand to the other. At the same time, he sang a song that was meant to distract the other players. Once all the bets were made, the player stopped singing and held the stone in one hand. Another player then guessed which hand held the stone.

▲ Four sticks and a basket used in a Klamath (KLAM uhth) guessing game. Two of the sticks are thicker, and two are thinner. The aim was for one side to arrange the sticks in a pattern under the basket. A pattern might be thick, thin, thin, thick, for example. The other side guessed at the pattern.

The Plateau Indians had a similar game. Each of two teams had a set of two bones. One bone in the set was painted; the other was left unpainted. A player from the first team held one bone in each hand. Then a player from the other team guessed which hand held the painted bone.

Another Northwest coast guessing game involved 10 disks. One of the disks, called "the chief," had a special marking. A smooth mat was laid out on the ground, and the disks were placed on top. One player rolled the mat up around the disks and shook the bundle. Then he or she ripped the mat in half. The other player or players had to guess which half contained the chief.

Games of Skill

Plateau Indians also played games that taught or improved upon important skills. One was the hoop-and-pole game. In this game, players had to stop a rolling hoop by hitting it with a wooden pole or spear that was thrown from a distance. The hoop-and-pole game tested skills that were needed in hunting and war.

Other games of skill included foot races, wrestling, and archery matches. As with the hoop-and-pole game, these contests helped young men prepare for their roles as hunters and warriors.

UP IN THE AIR

Juggling was one of the amusements enjoyed by American Indians. The Chinook were especially good at juggling and could keep as many as seven pebbles in the air at once.

▲ These rings were used by Kwakiutl Indians as archery targets. Shooting competitions helped sharpen a man's skill with the bow and arrow, a very important weapon for hunting and warfare.

A CHANGING WAY OF LIFE

In 1778, the British explorer James Cook landed on the Northwest coast. Less than 30 years later, the expedition led by Meriwether Lewis and William Clark encountered the people of the Plateau **cultural** area. Even before these men arrived, Northwest coast Indians had heard about white people from their trading partners to the east. Before long, traditional customs and **rituals** that had lasted thousands of years were threatened.

In Search of Riches

At first, explorers visited Indian lands and passed through without incident. But as more people heard about the rich natural resources in these areas, threats to the traditional Indian ways of life began to increase.

When fur trappers and traders first came into Indian territory in the early 1800's, they dealt fairly with the Indians. Before long, however, the non-Indians felt that they could just take the Indians' land.

▲ A water color of a trading post, painted by Peter Petersen Tofft around 1860. The trading post was on the Flathead Indian Reservation in present-day Montana. It was run by the Hudson's Bay Company. Its main business in North America was the fur trade. The company's charter gave it complete control over the lands where it set up its trading posts—and even allowed the company to declare war on the Indians. The presence of the Hudson's Bay Company on Indian lands led to conflict.

THE PROBLEM OF OWNERSHIP

Settlers from Europe were familiar with systems in which one person or family owned a piece of land. Most American Indians, on the other hand, considered themselves caretakers of the land. Because the Indians had no concept that one person could own the land, they also had no idea that they had a right to sell it or give it away. Thus, when Indians "sold" land, they often believed they were only agreeing to let the whites use it. The Indians expected to continue hunting or farming there. When the settlers tried to keep the Indians off what the settlers now considered their property, fighting broke out.

Killing Tradition

Another group of non-Indians followed the trappers, miners, and traders into Indian territory. They were Christian missionaries (people sent by a religious group to convert others to that faith). The missionaries encouraged the Indians to abandon their traditional religions and raise their children as Christians. They also wanted Indians to farm instead of hunt, and for Indian men to cut their long hair and to take only one wife. Little by little, non-Indians were trying to make Indians live like white people.

In the late 1700's, the United States government began establishing Indian **reservations.** Indians were moved from their traditional homelands to areas set aside by the government. With their movements limited and their traditional hunting, fishing, and gathering sites stolen, the Indians found their traditional ways of life disappearing. It was made even more difficult for many of the Northwest coast peoples when the Canadian government outlawed **potlatches** and spirit dances in 1884. This ban was not lifted until 1951.

When Europeans came to the Indians' land, they also brought diseases with them. Such illnesses as smallpox did not previously exist among the Indians, and they had no way to fight the sickness. These kinds of diseases that were new to the Indians wiped out entire **tribes.**

▶ A Nez Perce Indian wearing an outfit like those worn by white cowboys of the time. By the end of the 1880's, some Indians of the Northwest coast and Plateau had abandoned traditional lifestyles and were working as cowboys.

HOLDING ON TO TRADITION

Indians of the Northwest coast and Plateau **cultural** areas have faced many losses. Despite this, they have worked to retain their culture and traditions.

▲ A Tlingit chief takes part in a Sun Dance in 2000. He is wearing traditional clothing, including a nose ornament, and carrying totem symbols. The Sun Dance is used by the Tlingit to make contact with the spirit world.

Making It Work

Although most Indian **tribes** have lost their traditional lands, they have retained their **sovereignty** (*SOV ruhn tee*). This means the tribes of the Northwest coast and Plateau cultural areas are considered independent nations and can govern themselves. Although they cannot fully follow their traditional ways of life, many tribes have found a way to keep their customs alive.

Two villages of the Haida, for example, built an economy based on the forest industry and commercial fishing. For these and other Haida villages, tourism and arts and crafts have also become important sources of income. The woodcrafts made by many of the Northwest coast tribes have contributed to the tribes' economies and have served to keep their traditions alive. Interestingly, such Indian crafts as **totem** poles have become symbols for the entire geographic area of the Pacific Northwest, not just for the Indian culture.

Plateau Indians, too, have made the most of what they have left. The Flathead Indian **Reservation** in Montana is home to a resort and timber business. The Nez Perce have retail stores at Lapwai *(lap way)*, in Idaho, where the tribe also processes forest products and quarries (cuts and removes) the limestone.

Although their children might be raised in a much less traditional society, Indians of the Northwest coast and Plateau cultural areas continue to teach their children the ways of their ancestors. Many children learn the traditional languages, stories, songs, and dances of their tribes. **Powwows** also help keep tradition alive. These festivals, held throughout the United States and Canada, feature singers and dancers from many different tribes. Performers wear traditional costumes and sing songs that have been passed down for hundreds of years. Cultural centers, such as the Tamástslikt *(tuh MUH slikt)* Cultural Institute in Pendleton, Oregon, are of growing importance. As long as the Indians of the Northwest coast and Plateau regions have someone to tell the story of their people, and another person to listen, their ways will not be lost.

▼ Tsimshian children before a totem pole. The totem poles found throughout their village serve as daily reminders of their heritage.

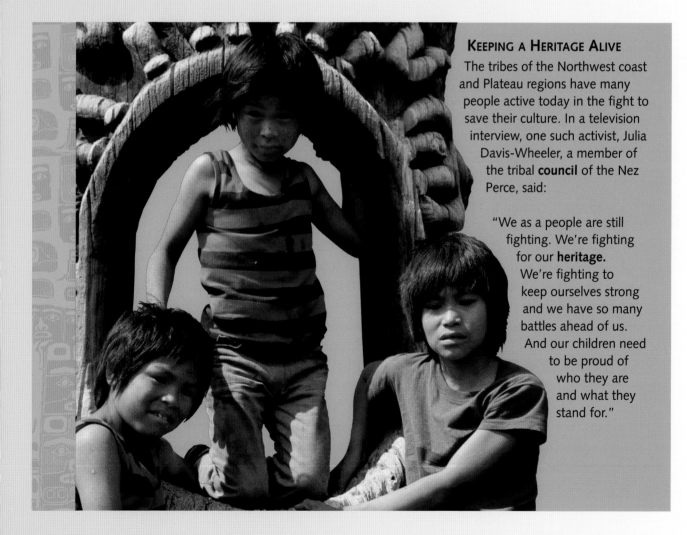

KEEPING A HERITAGE ALIVE

The tribes of the Northwest coast and Plateau regions have many people active today in the fight to save their culture. In a television interview, one such activist, Julia Davis-Wheeler, a member of the tribal **council** of the Nez Perce, said:

"We as a people are still fighting. We're fighting for our **heritage.** We're fighting to keep ourselves strong and we have so many battles ahead of us. And our children need to be proud of who they are and what they stand for."

GLOSSARY

archaeologist A scientist who studies the remains of past human cultures.

band A group of several extended families, related by blood or marriage, that lived in an area.

breechcloth A garment made up of a narrow band of cloth that was passed between the legs and looped over the front and rear of a belt.

bride price Gifts presented to the family of a future bride.

clan A group of people who are related through a common ancestor.

council A group of people called together to give advice and to discuss or settle questions.

cultural Having to do with a culture, or the way of life of a people. Culture includes a society's arts, beliefs, customs, institutions, inventions, language, technology, and values.

extended family A family that includes parents, children, grandparents, aunts, uncles, and cousins, all living together.

guardian spirit A spirit helper and teacher, often in the form of an animal, who guides a person.

harpoon An arrow-shaped weapon used to spear large fish and whales.

heritage That which is, or may be, handed on to a person from his or her ancestors, such as land, a trait, beliefs, or customs.

initiation ceremony A ceremony that marks a person's admission into a group or the passage from childhood to adulthood.

labret A lip ornament.

legend A folk story, often set in the past, which may be based in truth, but which may also contain fictional or fantastic elements. Legends are similar to myths, but myths often are about such sacred topics as gods or the creation of the world.

matrilineal Tracing family relationships and ancestry through the mother's side.

moiety Two sections of a single society; each half is a moiety. Clans in certain Indian groups were divided into moieties.

mortuary Of or having to do with death or burial.

Paleo-Indian A term for the earliest known human inhabitants of the Americas who lived from about 13,500 to 8,000 years ago.

patrilineal Tracing family relationships and ancestry through the father's side.

petroglyph A rock carving, usually a picture or symbol.

pictogram A picture symbol in certain writing systems that could be used to stand for an idea, a sound, or a name.

potlatch A ceremonial festival at which gifts are bestowed on the guests.

powwow A festival at which many different **tribes** meet and that features such performers as storytellers, singers, and dancers.

preserve Prepare food in such a way as to prevent it from spoiling.

puberty The physical beginning of manhood or womanhood.

radiocarbon dating A method used to determine the age of an object by measuring the amount of radiocarbon—or carbon 14—left in it.

reservation An area of land set aside and reserved for American Indians.

ritual A solemn or important act or ceremony, often religious in nature.

rockslide burial A method of burial; the deceased person's body is placed on a slope. Then, stones are piled upon the grave, or a rockslide is started that causes stones to slide onto the grave.

salmon run The period of time when salmon swim up the rivers in which they were born in order to spawn (reproduce).

shaman A person believed to have powers that come from direct contact with spirits.

sovereignty The right to govern oneself.

status Position, or rank, in a group or community.

sweat lodge A building heated so as to cause people inside it to perspire. Ceremonies held in a sweat lodge are used to purify the body, cure illnesses, and influence spirits.

totem A symbol—often an animal—of a **tribe, clan,** or family.

tree burial A method of burial by which a deceased person's body was placed in a wooden container. The container was then placed in a tree.

tribe A term that can mean a group made up of many clans that shared a territory and spoke a common language.

vision quest An **initiation ceremony** to help a person find his or her **guardian spirit.**

wager A bet, or anything which is risked, on the outcome of an event or the answer to a question.

weir A fence of stakes or broken branches, such as willow branches, put in a stream or channel. The Indians of the Northwest coast and Plateau used weirs to catch fish.

ADDITIONAL RESOURCES

Books

Encyclopedia of Native American Tribes
by Carl Waldman (Facts on File, 2006)

The Haida
by Raymond Bial (Benchmark Books, 2001)

Native Americans of the Northwest Plateau
by Kelly L. Barth (Lucent Books, 2002)

Native Tribes of the Great Basin and Plateau
by Michael Johnson and Duncan Clarke
(World Almanac Library, 2004)

Native Tribes of the North and Northwest Coast
by Michael Johnson and Jane Burkinshaw
(World Almanac Library, 2004)

The Nez Perce
by Raymond Bial (Benchmark Books, 2002)

The Tlingit
by Raymond Bial (Benchmark Books, 2003)

Web Sites

http://content.lib.washington.edu/aipnw/

http://www.manataka.org/page30.html

http://www.mnsu.edu/emuseum/cultural/northamerica/index.shtml

http://www.pbs.org/lewisandclark/native/index.html

INDEX

Acknowledgments

The Art Archive: 24, 37 (The British Library), 47 (Simplot Collection, gift of J.R. Simplot/Buffalo Bill Historical Center, Cody, Wyoming), 56 (Museum of Fine Arts, Boston), 57 (Bill Manns); **Bridgeman Art Library:** 12 (Peter Newark Pictures), 45 (Stapleton Collection); **Canadian Museum of Civilization** 55; **Corbis:** 5, 6 (Gunther Marx Photography), 9 (Stapleton Collection), 15 (Tim Thompson), 21 (Jan Butchofsky-Houser), 25 (Bettmann), 26 (Stapleton Collection), 32 (Macduff Everton), 38 (Historical Picture Archive), 39 (Michael Lewis), 42, 44 (Connie Rica), 49 (Edward S. Curtis), 51 (Edward S. Curtis), 54 (Burstein Collection), 58 (Louis Schwartzberg); **Library of Congress:** 17 (Edward S. Curtis), 36 (Edward S. Curtis), 48; **Werner Forman Archive:** 1 (Museum of Anthropology & Ethnography, St. Petersburg), 4 (University of British Columbia), 8 (Canadian Museum of Civilization), 10 (Royal Ontario Museum), 11 (Provincial Museum, Victoria, British Columbia), 13 (Museum of Anthropology & Ethnography, St. Petersburg), 14 (Provincial Museum, Victoria, British Columbia), 16 (James Hooper Collection, Watersfield, England), 18 (Private Collection, New York), 19 (Provincial Museum, Victoria, British Columbia), 20 (Museum of Anthropology & Ethnography, St. Petersburg), 22 (Portland Art Museum, Oregon), 23 (Field Museum of Natural History, Chicago), 27 (Museum of Anthropology, University of British Columbia), 28 (Museum of Anthropology, University of British Columbia), 29 (Terry R. Wills Collection, Ketchikan, Alaska), 30, 31 (Centennial Museum, Vancouver), 33, 34 (Museum of Anthropology & Ethnography, St. Petersburg), 35 (Provincial Museum, Victoria, British Columbia), 40 (Provincial Museum, Victoria, British Columbia), 41 (Field Museum of Natural History, Chicago), 43 (Canadian Museum of Civilization), 46 (Field Museum of Natural History, Chicago), 50 (Anthropological Museum of State University, Moscow), 52 (Provincial Museum, Victoria, British Columbia), 59.

Cover image: **Library of Congress**
Back cover image: **Shutterstock** (Joop Snijder, Jr.)